# SUMMER MATH WORKBOOK

## Bridge Building Activities

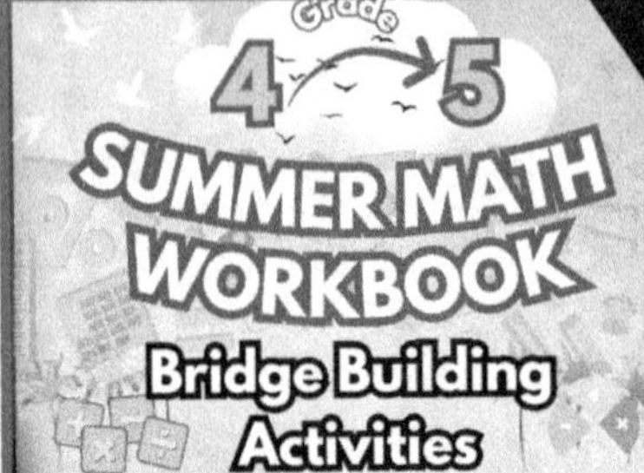


Grade
1 2
SUMMER MATH WORKBOOK
Bridge Building Activities
Number Sense
Addition and Subtraction
Place Value



Grade
2 3
SUMMER MATH WORKBOOK
Bridge Building Activities
Number Sense
Addition and Subtraction
Place Value



Grade
3 4
SUMMER MATH WORKBOOK
Bridge Building Activities
Number Sense
Addition and Subtraction
Place Value



Grade
4 5
SUMMER MATH WORKBOOK
Bridge Building Activities
Multiplication and Division
Place Value and Units
Fractions and Geometry



Grade
5 6
SUMMER MATH WORKBOOK
Bridge Building Activities
Multiplication and Division
Factors and Multiples
Fractions and Geometry



Grade
6 7
SUMMER MATH WORKBOOK
Bridge Building Activities
Arithmetic
Algebra
Geometry and Statistics



Grade
7 8
SUMMER MATH WORKBOOK
Bridge Building Activities
Ratio and Percentage
Algebra and Cartesian Plane
Geometry and Statistics



Grade
8 9
SUMMER MATH WORKBOOK
Bridge Building Activities
Ratio and Percentage
Algebra
Geometry and Graphing



Grade
9 10
SUMMER MATH WORKBOOK
Bridge Building Activities
Factoring and Distributing
Algebra
Geometry and Graphing

# <u>Introduction</u>

As parents and educators, we understand the pivotal role that mathematics plays in shaping a child's academic journey and future success. Yet, the path to mathematical proficiency can often seem daunting, filled with challenges and complexities. That's where the transformative power of Summer Bridge Building Activities books comes into play, illuminating the way forward with clarity, precision, and purpose.

Summer vacation is a time for rest and relaxation, but it also presents the risk of the "summer slide," where students lose some of the academic gains they made during the school year. Summer Bridge Building Activities books are specifically designed to tackle this challenge, ensuring that your child stays academically engaged and prepared for the upcoming school year. These books provide a seamless bridge from one grade to the next, reinforcing essential skills and introducing new concepts that will give your child a head start.

Imagine your child eagerly diving into the pages of a Summer Bridge Building Activities book, greeted by clear, engaging content that demystifies complex mathematical concepts. With each turn of the pages, they embark on a journey of discovery, encountering thoughtfully curated practice questions that reinforce learning and sharpen problem-solving skills. As they unveil the answers to those questions, a sense of accomplishment blossoms within them — a tangible reward for their hard work and dedication.

Summer Bridge Building Activities books transcend traditional educational tools; they are meticulously crafted to build a deep and enduring understanding of mathematics. These books follow a sequential and logical progression, starting from fundamental principles and advancing to sophisticated problem-solving strategies. Each chapter is designed to build on the previous one, ensuring a solid and comprehensive foundation for future learning.

Parents, we yearn for nothing more than to see our children thrive academically and personally. We want to witness the spark of inspiration ignited within them as they overcome academic challenges with confidence and poise. Summer Bridge Building Activities books serve as indispensable partners in this noble endeavor, offering not just practice questions but the keys to unlocking a world of academic and personal opportunities.

Visualize the pride on your child's face as they master a challenging math concept, the joy they experience when their efforts yield results, and the confidence they gain with each success. These pages are designed to make learning math a positive, enriching, and deeply rewarding experience that will benefit them throughout their academic journey and beyond.

For educators, Summer Bridge Building Activities books are invaluable allies in the quest to cultivate mathematical proficiency in the classroom. Accompanied by comprehensive guides and readily available answers, instructors can focus on mentoring and nurturing their students, secure in the knowledge that these books provide a robust framework for effective learning.

Within the pages of Summer Bridge Building Activities books lies not just the promise of academic excellence, but the seeds of a brighter future. By integrating these resources into your child's summer routine, you are bestowing upon them the gifts of confidence, curiosity, and a lifelong love of learning.

Invest in your child's future today with Summer Bridge Building Activities books — because every great journey begins with a single step, and this step can change everything. Keep the momentum of learning alive over the summer, and watch your child soar to new academic heights.

# Contents

Grade
7 - 9
PRE ALGEBRA
WORKBOOK
BRIDGE BUILDING
ACTIVITIES
Equations, Inequalities and Expressions
Linear Equations Graphing and Slope
System of Equations Quadratic Equations


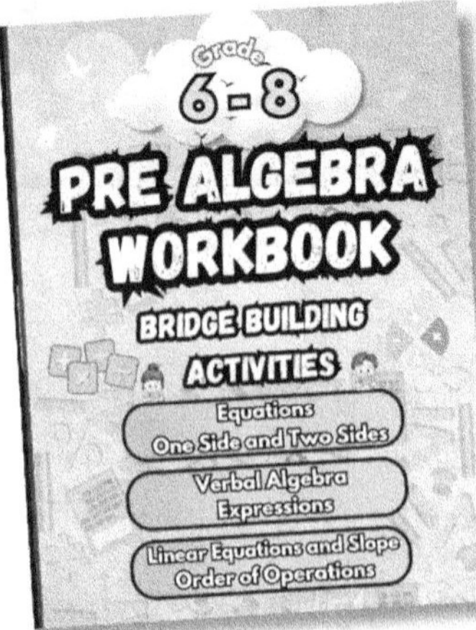

Grade
6 - 8
PRE ALGEBRA
WORKBOOK
BRIDGE BUILDING
ACTIVITIES
Equations One Side and Two Sides
Verbal Algebra Expressions
Linear Equations and Slope Order of Operations

Grade
5 - 6
PRE ALGEBRA
WORKBOOK
BRIDGE BUILDING
ACTIVITIES
Integers, Mixed Numbers Decimals and Fractions
Place Value Exponents and Roots
Percentage and Ratio Word Problems

PRE ALGEBRA
WORKBOOK
for
Beginners
Integers Fractions, Mixed Numbers
Place Value Exponents and Roots
Percentage Ratio Conversion

PRE ALGEBRA
WORKBOOK
for
Adults
Integers Percent and Ratio
Equations, Inequalities Expressions
Order of Operations


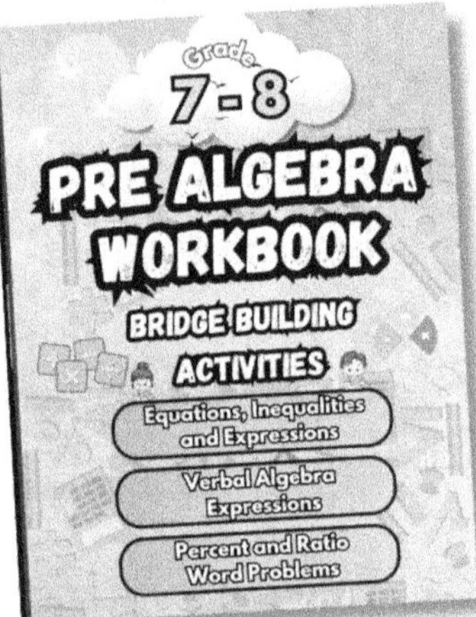

Grade
7 - 8
PRE ALGEBRA
WORKBOOK
BRIDGE BUILDING
ACTIVITIES
Equations, Inequalities and Expressions
Verbal Algebra Expressions
Percent and Ratio Word Problems

Grade
9 - 10
PRE ALGEBRA
WORKBOOK
BRIDGE BUILDING
ACTIVITIES
Equations and Inequalities Verbal Algebra
Linear and Quadratic Equations
System of Equations Polynomials

Grade
8th
ALGEBRA 1
WORKBOOK
BRIDGE BUILDING
ACTIVITIES
Order of Operations
One and Two Step Equations and Expressions
Linear Equations Cartesian Plane


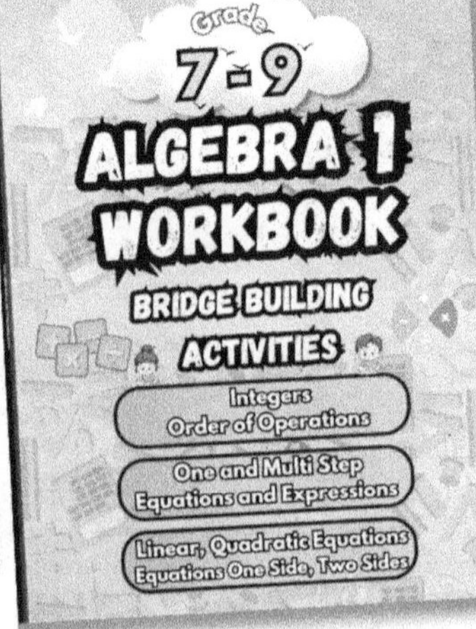

Grade
7 - 9
ALGEBRA 1
WORKBOOK
BRIDGE BUILDING
ACTIVITIES
Integers Order of Operations
One and Multi Step Equations and Expressions
Linear, Quadratic Equations Equations One Side, Two Sides

## Operations with Integers

Positive and negative integers are whole numbers that can represent quantities greater than zero and less than zero, respectively.

**Positive Integers:** Positive integers are whole numbers greater than zero. They are denoted by the numbers 1,2,3,4...

**Negative Integers:** Negative integers are whole numbers less than zero. They are denoted by placing a negative sign ("-") before the numbers, such as $-1,-2,-3,-4,...$

The positive integers are used to represent the number of objects, scores, etc. whereas the negative integers can be used to represent debt, losses, temperatures below freezing points, etc.

**Let's solve some problems:**

### 1. $6 - (-8) - 9$

- Start by simplifying within the parentheses:
$$-(-8) \text{ becomes } 8.$$
- Rewrite the expression with the simplified part:
$$6 + 8 - 9.$$
- Now perform addition and subtraction from left to right:
$$6 + 8 = 1\ 4, \text{ then } 14 - 9 = 5$$

### 2. $(-5) - (-3) + 10$

$$(-5) + 3 + 10$$

$$(-5) + 3 = -2, \text{ then } -2 + 10 = 8$$

## Operations with Integers

Evaluate Expressions.

**1)** $(-4) + 7 =$

**2)** $(-2) - (-5) + 6 =$

**3)** $8 - 8 + 4 =$

**4)** $3 - 9 + 5 =$

**5)** $(-5) - 8 =$

**6)** $(-7) - (-9) + 9 =$

**7)** $10 + 7 - 10 =$

**8)** $9 - 5 + 9 =$

**9)** $(-5) - (-6) =$

**10)** $9 - 4 + (-2) =$

**11)** $(-5) + 9 + (-6) =$

**12)** $(-1) - 9 =$

**13)** $8 + (-4) - 1 =$

**14)** $(-7) + 4 =$

**15)** $6 - 10 - 6 =$

**16)** $(-8) + (-3) =$

**17)** $9 - (-5) =$

**18)** $3 + (-9) + 4 =$

**19)** $(-3) + 6 =$

**20)** $(-5) - 10 + (-6) =$

**21)** $7 + 9 - 7 =$

**22)** $5 - (-2) - 6 =$

**23)** $6 - 2 + 6 =$

**24)** $(-3) - (-5) =$

**25)** $7 - 8 + 6 =$

**26)** $(-7) + 4 + (-7) =$

**27)** $3 - 5 + 5 =$

**28)** $7 + 4 - 2 =$

**29)** $(-2) - 1 =$

**30)** $1 - 4 - 1 =$

**31)** $10 + (-10) + 9 =$

**32)** $5 - (-7) =$

**33)** $6 - 3 + (-9) =$

**34)** $7 - 6 + 5 =$

**35)** $(-8) - (-10) + 8 =$

**36)** $(-10) + 5 =$

**37)** $(-9) - (-3) =$

**38)** $(-7) - (-7) - (-3) =$

# Exponents

An exponent tells us how many times a number (called the base) is multiplied by itself. It is written as a superscript to the right of the base number. For example, in $2^3$, 2 is the base and 3 is the exponent.

**Rules:**

1. **Product Rule**: When multiplying powers with the same base, add the exponents.

$$a^m \times a^n = a^{m+n}$$

For example:

$$2^3 = 2 \times 2 \times 2 = 8$$

$$3^2 \times 3^4 = 3^{2+4} = 3^6 = 3 \times 3 \times 3 \times 3 \times 3 \times 3 = 729$$

2. **Quotient Rule**: When dividing powers with the same base, subtract the exponents.

$$a^m \div a^n = a^{m-n}$$

For example:

$$5^3 \div 5^2 = 5^{3-2} = 5^1 = 5$$

3. **Power of a Power Rule**: When raising a power to another power, multiply the exponents.

$$(a^m)^n = a^{mn}$$

For example:

$$(2^2)^3 = 2^{2 \times 3} = 26 = 64$$

4. **Power of a Product Rule**: When raising a product to a power, distribute the power to each factor.

$$(ab)^n = a^n \times b^n$$

For example:

$$(2 \times 3)^2 = 2^2 \times 3^2 = 4 \times 9 = 36$$

5. **Power of a Quotient Rule**: When raising a quotient to a power, distribute the power to the numerator and denominator separately.

$$\left(\frac{a}{b}\right)^n = \frac{a^n}{b^n}$$

For example:

$$\left(\frac{4}{2}\right)^3 = \frac{4^3}{2^3} = \frac{64}{8} = 8$$

6. **Zero Exponent Rule**: Any nonzero number raised to the power of zero equals 11.

$$a^0 = 1$$

For example:

$$7^0 = 1$$

7. **Negative Exponent Rule**: A negative exponent means the reciprocal of the base raised to the positive exponent.

$$a^{-n} = \frac{1}{a^n}$$

For example:

$$2^{-3} = \frac{1}{2^3} = \frac{1}{8}$$

To evaluate expressions with exponents, we can use:

- **Repeated Multiplication**: Perform the multiplication indicated by the exponent.

**Exponents**

Convert the values.

1) $20^{-3}$ = _______________

2) $4^{-2}$ = _______________

3) $5^{-2}$ = _______________

4) $10^2$ = _______________

5) $11^{-3}$ = _______________

6) $15^{-2}$ = _______________

7) $3^{-2}$ = _______________

8) $4^4$ = _______________

9) $18^3$ = _______________

10) $18^4$ = _______________

11) $12^3$ = _______________

12) $8^{-2}$ = _______________

**13)** $1^3 =$ ___________

**14)** $13^{-2} =$ ___________

**15)** $19^{-2} =$ ___________

**16)** $1^{-2} =$ ___________

**17)** $16^{-3} =$ ___________

**18)** $9^2 =$ ___________

**19)** $14^4 =$ ___________

**20)** $8^4 =$ ___________

**21)** $17^3 =$ ___________

**22)** $15^2 =$ ___________

**23)** $20^4 =$ ___________

**24)** $5^4 =$ ___________

25) $13^2 =$ ___________

26) $19^{-3} =$ ___________

27) $20^3 =$ ___________

28) $17^2 =$ ___________

29) $17^{-3} =$ ___________

30) $5^{-3} =$ ___________

31) $14^{-2} =$ ___________

32) $6^{-3} =$ ___________

33) $10^{-2} =$ ___________

34) $11^4 =$ ___________

35) $4^{-3} =$ ___________

36) $17^{-2} =$ ___________

- **Using the Rules of Exponents**: Apply the appropriate rule to simplify expressions involving exponents.

## Square Roots

The square root of a number is a value that, when multiplied by itself, gives the original number. It's denoted by the symbol $\sqrt{\phantom{x}}$.

For example, the square root of 9 is 3 because 3 * 3 = 9.

## Cube Roots

The cube root of a number is a value that, when multiplied by itself twice, gives the original number. It's denoted by the symbol $\sqrt[3]{\phantom{x}}$.

For example, the cube root of 8 is 2 because 2 * 2 * 2 = 8.

## Square and Cube Roots

Calculate the root of each value.

1) $\sqrt[3]{8}$ = _______________

2) $\sqrt{4}$ = _______________

3) $\sqrt[3]{6,859}$ = _______________

4) $\sqrt[4]{16}$ = _______________

5) $\sqrt[3]{4,913}$ = _______________

6) $\sqrt[3]{1}$ = _______________

7) $\sqrt{361}$ = _______________

8) $\sqrt[3]{1,331}$ = _______________

9) $\sqrt[3]{2,197}$ = _______________

10) $\sqrt[4]{1,296}$ = _______________

11) $\sqrt[3]{3,375}$ = _______________

12) $\sqrt[3]{1,000}$ = _______________

13) $\sqrt[3]{4{,}096} = $ ___________

14) $\sqrt[3]{729} = $ ___________

15) $\sqrt{7{,}396} = $ ___________

16) $\sqrt[3]{216} = $ ___________

17) $\sqrt{3{,}481} = $ ___________

18) $\sqrt[4]{256} = $ ___________

19) $\sqrt{1{,}936} = $ ___________

20) $\sqrt[4]{1} = $ ___________

21) $\sqrt[3]{125} = $ ___________

22) $\sqrt{2{,}401} = $ ___________

23) $\sqrt[4]{10{,}000} = $ ___________

24) $\sqrt{49} = $ ___________

25) $\sqrt{729} = $ ___________

26) $\sqrt{36} = $ ___________

27) $\sqrt[3]{64}$ = _______________

28) $\sqrt{16}$ = _______________

29) $\sqrt[4]{4,096}$ = _______________

30) $\sqrt{961}$ = _______________

31) $\sqrt[3]{27}$ = _______________

32) $\sqrt{9}$ = _______________

33) $\sqrt[3]{5,832}$ = _______________

34) $\sqrt[4]{81}$ = _______________

35) $\sqrt{81}$ = _______________

36) $\sqrt[3]{10,648}$ = _______________

37) $\sqrt{676}$ = _______________

38) $\sqrt{9,216}$ = _______________

39) $\sqrt{196}$ = _______________

40) $\sqrt{3,969}$ = _______________

## Percentage

Percentage is a way of expressing a number as a fraction of 100. It is commonly used to represent proportions, rates, and comparisons. The symbol "%" is used to denote percentages.

To calculate a percentage, we multiply the given number by the appropriate fraction or decimal equivalent.

**How to calculate a percentage:**

**Convert Percentage to Decimal:** If the percentage is given as a percentage value (e.g., 25%), convert it to its decimal equivalent by dividing by 100.

$$\text{For example, 25\% as a decimal is } \frac{25}{100} = 0.25$$

**Multiply:** Multiply the decimal equivalent of the percentage by the given number. This gives us the portion of the number that represents the percentage.

$$100 \times 0.25 = 25\%$$

**Result:** The result is the calculated percentage value.

For example, to calculate 25% of 80:

Convert 25% to a decimal: 25% = 0.25.

Multiply 0.25 by 80: $0.25 \times 80 = 20$. The result is 20.

## Percentage

Find the percentage of given numbers.

**1)** 300% of 800 = ☐

**2)** 7% of ☐ = 35

**3)** 6% of 900 = ☐

**4)** 40% of ☐ = 80

**5)** 100% of ☐ = 700

**6)** 80% of ☐ = 32

**7)** ☐ of 400 = 800

**8)** ☐ of 600 = 180

**9)** 1% of 30 = ☐

**10)** ☐ of 100 = 25

11) 20% of 100 = ☐

12) ☐ of 400 = 8

13) 50% of ☐ = 150

14) 10% of ☐ = 8

15) 3% of ☐ = 27

16) ☐ of 800 = 800

17) 300% of 600 = ☐

18) 5% of 500 = ☐

19) 35% of 90 = ☐

20) 40% of 600 = ☐

21) ☐ of 500 = 30

22) 9% of ☐ = 81

23) 4% of ☐ = 20

24) 80% of ☐ = 16

25) 90% of ☐ = 180

26) ☐ of 500 = 300

27) 70% of 400 = ☐

28) 15% of ☐ = 15

29) 8% of ☐ = 48

30) 75% of 200 = ☐

## Percent Word Problems

Percent word problems involve situations where percentages are used to calculate quantities or amounts. These problems often require converting percentages to decimals and then applying them to the given values.

**For example:**

Bella bought a pair of shoes for $90.00. If she paid an additional 90% for taxes, how much in total did she pay for the shoes?

Given:

- Bella bought a pair of shoes for $90.00.

- She paid an additional 90% for taxes.

Calculate 90% of $90:

Tax= 90% × 90

Tax= 0.90 × 90

Tax= $81

Add the tax amount to the original price:

Total cost= $90 + $81

Total cost= $171

**Percent Word Problems**

1) A store has 40 desks. If 45% of them are sold at the end of the day, how many desks are sold?

2) Cooper had 80 bananas. He gave away 70% of them. How many did he have left?

3) In a school of 76 students, 25% of them take the bus to school. How many students take the bus?

4) In a survey of 24 people, 25% said they prefer cats over dogs. How many people prefer cats?

**5)** A store increases the prices of all items by 22%. If the socks originally costs $100.00, what is the sale price?

**6)** A person wants to make a 25% tip on a $76.00 meal. How much should the tip be?

**7)** In a basket of 20 thermometers, 95% are red thermometers . How many are red thermometers?

**8)** Zara bought bats for $80.00. If she paid an additional 45% for sales tax, how much in total did she pay for the bats?

**9)** In a class of 40 students, 5% of them are in the Math Club. How many students are in the Math Club?

**10)** Charlotte bought a shoes for $4.00. If she paid an additional 25% for sales tax, how much in total did she pay for the shoes?

**11)** Zoey had a collection of 60 baseball cards. She gave away 45% of them. How many did she have left?

**12)** In a class of 20 students, 95% are girls. How many are girls?

**13)** A classroom has 40 students, of which 45% are girls. How many boys are in the classroom?

**14)** Isaac buys medicines for $40.00 to sell them in market. If he wants to earn 70% profit. What must be the selling price of medicines?

**15)** A store is having a sale where everything is 25% off. The phones originally priced at $100.00 is now on sale. How much is the new price of phones now?

**16)** A school has 60 students. If 5% of them play baseball, how many students play baseball?

**17)** A company wants to increase its revenue by 82%. If its current revenue is $50.00 million, what should be its new revenue?

**18)** A school has 40 students. If 5% of them play tennis, how many students play tennis?

**19)** Jackson earned $80.00 for a week's work. If he paid 5% of it in taxes how much did he pay in taxes?

**20)** A store offers 70% discount on all products. If the sale price of cameras was 80, what was the original price?

# Ratio and Proportion Word Problems

We can use the concept of proportionality in solving many word problems, for example:

If a car travels 620 miles in six hours, how far can it travel in 12 hours?

Since the car travels a certain distance in a certain amount of time, we can assume that the distance traveled is directly proportional to the time taken.

Let $d$ be the distance the car can travel in 12 hours.

We can set up a proportion:

$$\frac{\text{Distance1}}{\text{Time1}} = \frac{\text{Distance2}}{\text{Time2}}$$

Substituting the given values:

$$\frac{620 \text{ miles}}{6 \text{ hours}} = \frac{d}{12 \text{ hours}}$$

Now, let's solve for $d$:

$$d = \frac{620 \times 12}{6} = \frac{7440}{6} = 1240$$

So, the car can travel 1240 miles in 12 hours.

## Ratio and Proportion Word Problems

1) If eight workers can build a house in 20 hours, how many workers are needed to build the house in five hours?

2) A school has a ratio of two teachers for every 27 students. If the school has 190 students, how many teachers are there?

3) A class has a ratio of four girls to every 10 boys. If there are 23 boys, how many girls are there?

**4)** If a recipe calls for two cups of water for every four cups of rice, how much water is needed for 10 cups of rice?

**5)** In a classroom, the ratio of boys to girls is three:nine. If there are 17 girls, how many boys are there?

**6)** Madelyn sells five headphones for every six Gloves. If there are 74 headphones, how many Gloves are there?

**7)** A grocery store has a ratio of four apples to every 10 oranges. If there are 50 oranges in the store, how many apples are there?

**8)** A charity received a donation of $1,422 from a company. If the donation was divided among five charities in the ratio 2:3:4:5:6, how much did the fifth charity receive?

**9)** A car can travel 30 miles per gallon of gas. How many gallons of gas are needed to travel 197 miles?

**10)** If it takes six students 16 hours to complete a science project, how many students are needed to finish the project in eight hours?

**11)** In a bag of candies, the ratio of chocolate candies to fruit candies is four:10. If there are 12 fruit candies, how many chocolate candies are there?

**12)** If nine workers can complete a job in 17 days, how many workers are needed to complete the job in seven days?

NAME: _______________

**13)** If a recipe calls for two eggs for every 10 cups of flour, how many eggs are needed for 14 cups of flour?

**14)** A school has a ratio of two female teachers to every seven male teachers. If there are 28 male teachers, how many female teachers are there?

**15)** A bus travels at a speed of 87 miles per hour. How long will it take to travel 151 miles?

**16)** A charity received a donation of $2,367 from a company. If the donation was divided among five charities in the ratio 2:3:4:5:6, how much did the fourth charity receive?

**17)** If a recipe calls for one teaspoon of salt for every six cups of flour, how much salt is needed for 14 cups of flour?

**18)** If four chefs can bake 100 cakes in 20 hours, how many chefs are needed to bake the same number of cakes in five hours?

**19)** If a car travels 352 miles in four hours, how far can it travel in 11 hours?

**20)** A machine can produce 182 units of a product in eight hours. How long will it take to produce 364 units?

**21)** A company has a ratio of three female employees to every six male employees. If there are 22 male employees, how many female employees are there?

# Order of Operations (PEMDAS)

The order of operations, often remembered by the acronym PEMDAS, stands for:

- **Parentheses**: Perform operations inside parentheses first.
- **Exponents**: Evaluate exponents (powers and roots) next.
- **Multiplication and Division**: Perform multiplication and division from left to right.
- **Addition and Subtraction:** Perform addition and subtraction from left to right.

The order of operations helps to clarify which operations should be performed first in a mathematical expression to ensure consistent and accurate results.

- **Parentheses**: Evaluate expressions within parentheses first. If there are nested parentheses, start with the innermost ones and work your way out.

    1. Example: $2 \times ( 3 + 4) = 2 \times 7 = 14$

- **Exponents**: Evaluate expressions with exponents (powers and roots) next.

    1. Example: $2^3 + 4 = 8 + 4 = 12$

- **Multiplication and Division**: Perform multiplication and division from left to right.

    1. Example: $2 \times 3 + 4 = 6 + 4 = 10$

    2. Example: $6 \div 2 \times 3 = 3 \times 3 = 9$

- **Addition and Subtraction**: Perform addition and subtraction from left to right.

    1. Example: $2 + 3 \times 4 = 2 + 12 = 14$

    2. Example: $10 - 4 \div 2 = 10 - 2 = 8$

## Order of Operations (PEMDAS)

**1)** $10(3 + 2) =$

**2)** $(2^2) \times (4^2) + 6 =$

**3)** $5 + 6^2 =$

**4)** $(4 + 1)^2 =$

**5)** $(9 + 2)^2 =$

**6)** $(4 + 3) \div 5 =$

**7)** $4 \times (6 + 5) =$

**8)** $2 \times 1 =$

**9)** $(10 \times 9) - (10 + 2) =$

**10)** $6 + 8 + 6 + 8 =$

**11)** $(3 + 3)^2 + (9 + 5)^2 =$

**12)** $10 \times (7 + 4) =$

**13)** $6 \times 5 \times 10 =$

**14)** $6(3 + 1) =$

**15)** $4 + 1 + 7 =$

**16)** $(6^2) \times (7^2) + 10 =$

**17)** $(5^2) \times (4^2) + 7 =$

**18)** $9 + 1 + 4 + 1 =$

**19)** $(7 + 2) \times (3 + 1) =$

**20)** $6 \times 6 \times 10 =$

**21)** $7 \times 4 \times 2 =$

**22)** $(3 + 5) \div 3 =$

**23)** $(8 + 10) \times (10 + 9) =$

**24)** $6 + 10 + 10 + 10 =$

**25)** $7 + 9^2 + 4 + 6^2 =$

**26)** $(10 \times 9) - (2 + 5) =$

**27)** $(6 + 4)^2 =$

**28)** $8(1 + 9) =$

**29)** $10 \times 3 =$

**30)** $(4^2) \times (5^2) + 4 =$

**31)** $10 \times 3 + 5 =$

**32)** $1 \times 9 \times 4 =$

**33)** $(2 \times 4) - (3 + 5) =$

**34)** $5(9 + 4) =$

**35)** $(2 + 4)(2 + 1) =$

**36)** $3(9 + 5) =$

**37)** $(7^2) \times (7^2) + 8 =$

**38)** $3 \times 9 \times 9 =$

**39)** $6 + 4^2 =$

**40)** $5 + 8 - 7 + 6 =$

## Multiple Operations Fractions

Fraction multiple operations involve performing multiple arithmetic operations (addition, subtraction, multiplication, division) on fractions.

We follow (PEDMAS that stands for the order of operations in arithmetic) to solve multiple operations Fractions:

1. **Parentheses:** Perform operations inside parentheses first.

2. **Exponents:** Evaluate expressions with exponents or powers.

3. **Multiplication and Division:** Perform multiplication and division from left to right.

4. **Addition and Subtraction:** Perform addition and subtraction from left to right.

**For example:**

Let's solve the expression: $\frac{3}{4} + \frac{1}{2} \times \frac{2}{3}$

**Step 1:** Begin by performing the multiplication operation first:

$$= \frac{1 \times 2}{2 \times 4} = \frac{2}{6} = \frac{1}{3}$$

**Step 2:** Now rewrite the expression with the result of the multiplication:

$$\frac{3}{4} + \frac{1}{3}$$

**Step 3:** To add fractions, find a common denominator. In this case, the least common multiple (LCM) of 4 and 3 is 12.

**Step 4:** Rewrite both fractions with the common denominator:

$$\frac{9}{12} + \frac{4}{12}$$

**Step 5:** Add the numerators together and keep the common denominator:

$$\frac{13}{12} = 1\frac{1}{12}$$

## Multiple Operations Fractions

Find the solution.

**1)** $\left(\frac{1}{6} + \frac{3}{5}\right) - \left(\frac{3}{5} \times \frac{1}{4}\right) =$

**2)** $\frac{2}{3} + \frac{2}{9} + \frac{1}{9} =$

**3)** $\left(\frac{1}{3} + \frac{3}{5}\right) \times \left(\frac{3}{8} + \frac{2}{5}\right) =$

**4)** $\left(\frac{3}{4} + \frac{1}{2}\right) \div \frac{3}{5} =$

**5)** $\frac{1}{2} + \frac{1}{7} + 9 =$

**6)** $\left(\frac{1}{4} + \frac{6}{7}\right) - \left(\frac{7}{10} \times \frac{3}{10}\right) =$

**7)** $\frac{1}{8} + \frac{5}{8} + 2 =$

**8)** $\frac{1}{4} \times \frac{2}{3} + \frac{4}{9} =$

**9)** $\dfrac{3}{10} \times \dfrac{1}{4} \times \dfrac{1}{8} =$

**10)** $\dfrac{1}{4} \times \dfrac{4}{5} \times \dfrac{1}{6} =$

**11)** $\left(\dfrac{5}{9} + \dfrac{3}{7}\right) - \left(\dfrac{2}{9} \times \dfrac{2}{3}\right) =$

**12)** $\dfrac{4}{7} + \dfrac{9}{10} + \dfrac{1}{3} + \dfrac{1}{4} =$

**13)** $\dfrac{2}{3} + \dfrac{3}{7} + \dfrac{2}{3} =$

**14)** $\left(\dfrac{1}{6} + \dfrac{1}{7}\right) \div \dfrac{1}{3} =$

**15)** $\dfrac{5}{8} + \dfrac{1}{4} + 2 =$

**16)** $\dfrac{2}{3} + \dfrac{3}{4} + \dfrac{2}{9} =$

**17)** $\left(\dfrac{2}{5} + \dfrac{1}{4}\right) \times \left(\dfrac{2}{9} + \dfrac{4}{5}\right) =$

**18)** $\left(\dfrac{3}{8} \times \dfrac{6}{7}\right) + \left(\dfrac{1}{2} \times \dfrac{5}{7}\right) =$

**19)** $\dfrac{5}{8} + \dfrac{2}{3} + 4 =$

**20)** $\left(\dfrac{1}{4} + \dfrac{1}{4}\right) - \left(\dfrac{3}{5} \times \dfrac{1}{4}\right) =$

**21)** $\left(\dfrac{3}{10} \times \dfrac{1}{6}\right) + \left(\dfrac{3}{5} \times \dfrac{1}{4}\right) =$

# Mixed Numbers: Mixed into Improper

Mixed numbers and improper fractions are two different ways to represent the same value of a fraction.

1. **Mixed Number:** A mixed number is a combination of a whole number and a proper fraction. For example, $2\frac{1}{3}$ is a mixed number, where 2 is the whole number part and $\frac{1}{3}$ is the fraction part.

2. **Improper Fraction:** An improper fraction is a fraction where the numerator is greater than or equal to the denominator. For example, $\frac{7}{3}$ is an improper fraction because 6 is greater than 3.

To convert a mixed number to an improper fraction, you multiply the whole number by the denominator of the fraction, add the numerator, and then write the result over the original denominator. For example:

$$2\frac{1}{3} = \frac{2 \times 3 + 1}{3} = \frac{7}{3}$$

To convert an improper fraction to a mixed number, we divide the numerator by the denominator. The quotient becomes the whole number part, and the remainder becomes the numerator of the fraction. For example:

$$\frac{7}{3} = 2\frac{1}{3}$$

# Mixed Numbers: Addition and Subtraction

To add or subtract mixed numbers, we follow similar steps as when adding or subtracting regular fractions. For instance:

## Addition:

- <u>Add the whole numbers:</u> Add the whole number parts of the mixed numbers together.
- <u>Add the fractions:</u> Add the fractions parts of the mixed numbers together.
- <u>Simplify (if needed):</u> If the fraction part of the sum is an improper fraction, simplify it by converting it to a mixed number.

## Subtraction:

- <u>Subtract the whole numbers:</u> Subtract the whole number part of the second mixed number from the whole number part of the first mixed number.
- <u>Subtract the fractions:</u> Subtract the fraction part of the second mixed number from the fraction part of the first mixed number.
- <u>Simplify (if needed):</u> If the fraction part of the difference is a negative fraction, borrow from the whole number part or simplify it by converting it to a mixed number.

# Mixed Numbers: Multiplication and Division

To multiply or divide mixed numbers, we follow these steps:

## Multiplication:

- <u>Convert the mixed numbers to improper fractions:</u> Multiply the whole number by the denominator of the fraction, then add the numerator. Write the result over the original denominator.
- <u>Multiply the fractions:</u> Multiply the numerators together to get the new numerator and multiply the denominators together to get the new denominator.
- <u>Simplify (if needed):</u> If the result is an improper fraction, simplify it by converting it back to a mixed number.

## Division:

- <u>Convert the mixed numbers to improper fractions:</u>
- <u>Invert the divisor:</u> Flip the second fraction (the one you're dividing by) so that the division becomes multiplication.
- <u>Multiply the fractions:</u> Multiply the numerators together to get the new numerator and multiply the denominators together to get the new denominator.
- <u>Simplify (if needed):</u> If the result is an improper fraction, simplify it by converting it back to a mixed number.

## Mixed Numbers

Calculate.

1) $8\frac{2}{8} - 7\frac{1}{2} = $ _______________

2) $7\frac{7}{9} + 9\frac{1}{3} = $ _______________

3) $8\frac{2}{8} - 5\frac{2}{5} = $ _______________

4) $8\frac{1}{2} - 5\frac{4}{7} = $ _______________

5) $2\frac{5}{6} \div 1\frac{9}{10} = $ _______________

**6)** $6\frac{1}{4} - 5\frac{1}{9} =$

**7)** $7\frac{3}{5} - 6\frac{5}{7} =$

**8)** $8\frac{8}{10} \times 6\frac{1}{2} =$

**9)** $2\frac{2}{6} - 1\frac{2}{4} =$

**10)** $1\frac{1}{3} \times 9\frac{2}{8} =$

**11)** $6\frac{8}{9} + 8\frac{1}{4} =$ ___________________

**12)** $7\frac{1}{3} - 4\frac{6}{9} =$ ___________________

**13)** $8\frac{1}{2} + 9\frac{3}{8} =$ ___________________

**14)** $5\frac{4}{5} \div 2\frac{3}{7} =$ ___________________

**15)** $1\frac{4}{6} \div 8\frac{7}{10} =$ ___________________

**16)** $1\frac{3}{5} \div 7\frac{1}{8} =$ ________________

**17)** $4\frac{1}{2} + 9\frac{5}{10} =$ ________________

**18)** $5\frac{1}{6} \times 2\frac{1}{9} =$ ________________

**19)** $8\frac{3}{4} - 4\frac{2}{3} =$ ________________

**20)** $2\frac{2}{7} \div 8\frac{3}{6} =$ ________________

**21)** $8\frac{2}{3} - 2\frac{7}{9} =$ _______________________

**22)** $4\frac{6}{7} + 8\frac{3}{8} =$ _______________________

**23)** $9\frac{1}{2} + 4\frac{2}{5} =$ _______________________

**24)** $9\frac{2}{10} - 5\frac{3}{4} =$ _______________________

**25)** $8\frac{1}{7} \times 5\frac{3}{5} =$ _______________________

## Solving One-Step Equations

Solving one-step equations involves finding the value of the variable that makes the equation true. In a one-step equation, there is only one operation (addition, subtraction, multiplication, or division) performed on the variable.

The goal is to isolate the variable on one side of the equation by performing inverse operations.

### For example:

Given the equation $6 = -3z$, where we want to solve for z.

The given equation is already in the form of a one-step equation, with z being multiplied by $-3$.

To isolate z, we need to perform the inverse operation of multiplication, which is division.

Divide both sides by $-3$:

$$\frac{6}{-3} = \frac{-3z}{-3}$$

Simplify:

$$-2 = z$$

So, the solution to the equation is $z = -2$.

When we substitute the value of $z = -2$ back into the original equation, $6 = -3(-2)$, it simplifies to $6 = 6$. This confirms that our solution is correct because it satisfies the original equation.

## Solving One-Step Equations

Solve for the variable.

**1)** $0.1 = 1 \div k$

**2)** $s \times 5 + 9 = 39$

**3)** $12 = (1 \times y) + 3$

**4)** $7 + a = 11$

**5)** $1 \times (x - 10) = -7$

**6)** $4k + 3 = 39$

**7)** $45 = 3(6 + m)$

**8)** $54 = 5 \times b + b$

**9)** $11 = 2 + a$

**10)** $16 = a \times 4 - 8$

**11)** $7m + m = 72$

**12)** $5 = 6k - k$

**13)** $2y - 9 = -7$

**14)** $35 = (4 \times m) + 3$

**15)** $10 + (5 \times y) = 55$

**16)** $s + 3 = 11$

**17)** $10 = a \times 1 + 6$

**18)** $2 + (1 \times m) = 12$

**19)** $(b \div 1) + b = 8$

**20)** $a \times 8 - 2 = 22$

**21)** $m + 3 = 12$

**22)** $5 + y = 6$

**23)** $s \times 1 - 1 = 9$

**24)** $a \times 1 + 8 = 12$

**25)** $6(2 - a) = -48$

**26)** $28 = x \times 7 - 7$

**27)** $6 + (4 \times b) = 42$

**28)** $8 + (k - 7) = 10$

**29)** $6 + b = 14$

**30)** $9 \times (k - 3) = -18$

**31)** $(8 \div b) + 6 = 7$

**32)** $s + 5 = 13$

33) $x \div 1 = 9$

34) $2.1 = 1 + (k \div 9)$

35) $m \times 8 + 6 = 70$

36) $18 = 9 + x$

37) $48 = 6 \times z$

38) $4a + a = 20$

39) $9(8 - s) = 27$

40) $10 + (a \div 8) = 11.1$

## Solving Equations (One Side)

Solving one-step equations involves performing a single operation to isolate the variable and find its value.

Let's solve an equation step by step: $16 + x = 31$

1.  Identify the Goal:

    The goal is to isolate the variable $x$ on one side of the equation.

2.  Simplify the Equation: Combine like terms on both sides of the equation, if necessary.

    The equation is already simplified.

3.  Undo Addition or Subtraction: If there's addition or subtraction involving the variable, undo it by performing the opposite operation on both sides of the equation.

    Since $x$ is being added to 16, we'll undo this operation by subtracting 16 from both sides of the equation:
    $$16 + x - 16 = 31 - 16$$

4.  Isolate the Variable: Ensure that the variable is alone on one side of the equation.

    $$x = 15$$

5.  Check Your Solution: Substitute the value of $x$ back into the original equation to verify that it satisfies the equation.

    $$16 + 15 = 31$$

    $$31 = 31$$

    The equation is balanced.

## Equations: (One Side)

Solve the equations for the variable.

**1)** $z + 2 = 10$

**2)** $6 - m = 16$

**3)** $-9 + y = 1$

**4)** $y - 11 = 5$

**5)** $3 + 9z = 21$

**6)** $x \div -2 = 10$

**7)** $m \times 2 = -16$

**8)** $76 - 18k = 4$

9) $-4 \times x = 36$

10) $-80 \div z = -10$

11) $-10 \times z = -40$

12) $x \times 5 = -50$

13) $9k + 10 = 109$

14) $k \times 12 = 132$

15) $6y - 16 = 92$

16) $18 - y = 23$

**17)** $13x + 12 = -118$

**18)** $8z - 2 = 126$

**19)** $-2 - z = 4$

**20)** $18m - 4 = 14$

**21)** $15 \times m = 285$

**22)** $11m - 15 = 51$

**23)** $2y + -2 = 8$

**24)** $z + -9 = -14$

**25)** $k - 8 = 8$

**26)** $k \times -3 = -9$

**27)** $-7 - -7k = 84$

**28)** $6 + -1x = -13$

**29)** $m \times -10 = 60$

**30)** $k - -9 = 23$

**31)** $0 \div k = 0$

**32)** $x - 4 = 2$

**33)** $9 + m = 8$

**34)** $k - 2 = 8$

**35)** $k \times 12 = -12$

**36)** $k + 3 = -5$

**37)** $-68 \div x = -4$

**38)** $m - -8 = 15$

**39)** $16 + k = 21$

**40)** $y + 18 = 17$

**41)** $19x + 19 = -171$

**42)** $z \div -10 = 2$

**43)** $-4m + -10 = -58$

**44)** $122 - 12y = 2$

**45)** $12 \div y = -3$

**46)** $4 + -10m = -166$

**47)** $k + 6 = 23$

**48)** $-3 + k = -9$

**49)**  $19 \times m = -114$

**50)**  $-6 \times k = -84$

**51)**  $17m - -9 = 77$

**52)**  $k \times 0 = 0$

**53)**  $x \div 14 = 18$

**54)**  $8 - -7m = 106$

**55)**  $k + 20 = 37$

**56)**  $1 + x = 12$

<u>**Evaluating Equations**</u>

Evaluating expressions involves substituting given values for variables in an expression and then performing the indicated operations to find the result.

For example: Let's evaluate  $4x - 10$, when $x = 3$:

Step 1: Substitute the given value for the variable:

Replace every occurrence of x in the expression $4x - 10$ with the given value, which is 3:

$$= 4(3) - 10$$

## Step 2: Perform the operations:

Perform the indicated operations according to the order of operations (PEMDAS - Parentheses, Exponents, Multiplication and Division, Addition and Subtraction):

$$= 4 \times 3 - 10$$

Step 3: Simplify:

Calculate the result:

$$12 - 10 = 2$$

## Evaluating Equations

Simplify the following equations when the value of $n = 3$

**1)** $1(n + 6) + n(10 - n) =$

**2)** $7n + 7 \times (n + 4) =$

**3)** $2n + 8 + (3n - 8) =$

**4)** $3n + 9 + (7n - 3) =$

**5)** $6n - n =$

**6)** $(6 \div n) + 8 =$

**7)** $10(n + 8) + (3n - 7) =$

**8)** $7 \times n + 6 =$

## Evaluating Equations

Simplify the following equations when the value of  n = 7

**1)**  $n + 9 + 3n =$

**2)**  $9 + (9n + 10) =$

**3)**  $9 \times (1 - n) =$

**4)**  $(6n + 8) \times (n - 5) =$

**5)**  $(5 - n) \times 8 =$

**6)**  $3n - 1 + n =$

**7)**  $n + 6 + 9n =$

**8)**  $10 \times n + n =$

# SUMMER ALGEBRA WORKBOOK
## BUILDING ACTIVITIES

## Evaluating Equations

Simplify the following equations when the value of $n = 2$

**1)** $n \times 10 + 7 =$

**2)** $6 \times (n - 3) =$

**3)** $9 \times n + n =$

**4)** $6n + n =$

**5)** $3 + 9n - n(4 + n) =$

**6)** $5 + (8n + 6) =$

**7)** $9 + 10n =$

**8)** $(2n)^1 =$

## Evaluating Equations

Simplify the following equations when the value of $n = 6$

1) $6n + n + 10n =$

2) $n \times 9 + 9 =$

3) $6 + (n \div 4) =$

4) $(8 - n) \times (5n + 7) =$

5) $n \times 1 =$

6) $9n - 3 + 2n =$

7) $(6 \times n) - 3 =$

8) $n + n =$

## Evaluating Equations

Simplify the following equations when the value of $n = 5$

**1)** $n \div 7 =$

**2)** $3(n + 3) + n(4 - n) =$

**3)** $n \times 8 + 5 =$

**4)** $n \times 7 =$

**5)** $9 \times n + n =$

**6)** $(8n)^1 =$

**7)** $9 + (7 \times n) =$

**8)** $n + 5 =$

## Evaluating Equations

Simplify the following equations when the value of $n = 2$

**1)** $10n + 7 =$

**2)** $(6n + 2) \times (n + 4) =$

**3)** $9n - n =$

**4)** $10 + (7n + 2) - 6 + (7n) =$

**5)** $9(3 + n) =$

**6)** $n + (9 \div n) =$

**7)** $2 + (5n - n)(2 + n) =$

**8)** $n + (10 \div n) =$

## Evaluating Equations

Simplify the following equations when the value of  n = 6

**1)**  $(n + 2) \times (n - 3) =$

**2)**  $n + (4 \div n) =$

**3)**  $n + 5 + 7n =$

**4)**  $n + 4 + 7n =$

**5)**  $(7 - n) \times (8n + 3) =$

**6)**  $(4 - n) \times 6 =$

**7)**  $(8 \times n) + 3 =$

**8)**  $7(3 - n) =$

# ANSWERS

**Page 1:  Operations with Integers**

**1.** 3 **2.** 9 **3.** 4 **4.** -1 **5.** -13 **6.** 11 **7.** 7 **8.** 13 **9.** 1

**10.** 3 **11.** -2 **12.** -10 **13.** 3 **14.** -3 **15.** -10 **16.** -11 **17.** 14 **18.** -2

**19.** 3 **20.** -21 **21.** 9 **22.** 1 **23.** 10 **24.** 2 **25.** 5 **26.** -10 **27.** 3

**28.** 9 **29.** -3 **30.** -4 **31.** 9 **32.** 12 **33.** -6 **34.** 6 **35.** 10 **36.** -5

**37.** -6 **38.** 3

**Page 5:  Exponents**

**1.** 1/8000 **2.** 1/16 **3.** 1/25 **4.** 100 **5.** 1/1331

**6.** 1/225 **7.** 1/9 **8.** 256 **9.** 5,832 **10.** 104,976

**11.** 1,728 **12.** 1/64 **13.** 1 **14.** 1/169 **15.** 1/361

**16.** 1 **17.** 1/4096 **18.** 81 **19.** 38,416 **20.** 4,096

**21.** 4,913 **22.** 225 **23.** 160,000 **24.** 625 **25.** 169

**26.** 1/6859 **27.** 8,000 **28.** 289 **29.** 1/4913 **30.** 1/125

**31.** 1/196 **32.** 1/216 **33.** 1/100 **34.** 14,641 **35.** 1/64

**36.** 1/289

**Page 8:  Square and Cube Roots**

**1.** 2 **2.** 2 **3.** 19 **4.** 2 **5.** 17 **6.** 1 **7.** 19 **8.** 11 **9.** 13

**10.** 6 **11.** 15 **12.** 10 **13.** 16 **14.** 9 **15.** 86 **16.** 6 **17.** 59 **18.** 4

**19.** 44 **20.** 1 **21.** 5 **22.** 49 **23.** 10 **24.** 7 **25.** 27 **26.** 6 **27.** 4

**28.** 4 **29.** 8 **30.** 31 **31.** 3 **32.** 3 **33.** 18 **34.** 3 **35.** 9 **36.** 22

**37.** 26     **38.** 96     **39.** 14     **40.** 63

## Page 11:   Percentage

**1.** 2400        **2.** 500        **3.** 54        **4.** 200        **5.** 700        **6.** 40        **7.** 200%

**8.** 30%        **9.** 0.3        **10.** 25%        **11.** 20        **12.** 2%        **13.** 300        **14.** 80

**15.** 900        **16.** 100%        **17.** 1800        **18.** 25        **19.** 31.5        **20.** 240        **21.** 6%

**22.** 900        **23.** 500        **24.** 20        **25.** 200        **26.** 60%        **27.** 280        **28.** 100

**29.** 600        **30.** 150

## Page 14:   Percent Word Problems

**1.** 18        **2.** 24        **3.** 19        **4.** 6        **5.** $122.00        **6.** $19.00

**7.** 19        **8.** $116.00        **9.** 2        **10.** $5.00        **11.** 33        **12.** 19

**13.** 22        **14.** $68.00        **15.** $75.00        **16.** 3        **17.** $91.00        **18.** 2

**19.** $4.00        **20.** 136

## Page 19:   Ratio and Proportion Word Problems

**1.** 32        **2.** 14.07        **3.** 9.2        **4.** 5        **5.** 5.67        **6.** 88.8

**7.** 20        **8.** 426.6        **9.** 6.57        **10.** 12        **11.** 4.8        **12.** 21.86

**13.** 2.8        **14.** 8        **15.** 1.74        **16.** 591.75        **17.** 2.33        **18.** 16

**19.** 968        **20.** 16        **21.** 11

## Page 26:   Order of Operations (PEMDAS)

**1.** 50        **2.** 70        **3.** 41        **4.** 25        **5.** 121        **6.** 1.4        **7.** 44

**8.** 2        **9.** 78        **10.** 28        **11.** 232        **12.** 110        **13.** 300        **14.** 24

**15.** 12        **16.** 1,774        **17.** 407        **18.** 15        **19.** 36        **20.** 360        **21.** 56

**22.** 2.7        **23.** 342        **24.** 36        **25.** 128        **26.** 83        **27.** 100        **28.** 80

**29.** 30      **30.** 404      **31.** 35      **32.** 36      **33.** 0      **34.** 65      **35.** 18

**36.** 42      **37.** 2,409      **38.** 243      **39.** 22      **40.** 12

## Page 30:   Multiple Operations Fractions

**1.** 37/60      **2.** 1      **3.** 217/300      **4.** 2 1/12      **5.** 9 9/14

**6.** 157/175      **7.** 2 3/4      **8.** 11/18      **9.** 3/320      **10.** 1/30

**11.** 158/189      **12.** 2 23/420      **13.** 1 16/21      **14.** 13/14      **15.** 2 7/8

**16.** 1 23/36      **17.** 299/450      **18.** 19/28      **19.** 5 7/24      **20.** 7/20

**21.** 1/5

## Page 35:   Mixed Numbers

**1.** 3/4      **2.** 17 1/9      **3.** 2 17/20      **4.** 2 13/14      **5.** 1 28/57

**6.** 1 5/36      **7.** 31/35      **8.** 57 1/5      **9.** 5/6      **10.** 12 1/3

**11.** 15 5/36      **12.** 2 2/3      **13.** 17 7/8      **14.** 2 33/85      **15.** 50/261

**16.** 64/285      **17.** 14      **18.** 10 49/54      **19.** 4 1/12      **20.** 32/119

**21.** 5 8/9      **22.** 13 13/56      **23.** 13 9/10      **24.** 3 9/20      **25.** 45 3/5

## Page 40:   Solving One-Step Equations

**1.** 10      **2.** 6      **3.** 9      **4.** 4      **5.** 3      **6.** 9      **7.** 9      **8.** 9      **9.** 9

**10.** 6      **11.** 9      **12.** 1      **13.** 1      **14.** 8      **15.** 9      **16.** 8      **17.** 4      **18.** 10

**19.** 4      **20.** 3      **21.** 9      **22.** 1      **23.** 10      **24.** 4      **25.** 10      **26.** 5      **27.** 9

**28.** 9      **29.** 8      **30.** 1      **31.** 8      **32.** 8      **33.** 9      **34.** 10      **35.** 8      **36.** 9

**37.** 8      **38.** 4      **39.** 5      **40.** 9

## Page 45:   Equations: (One Side)

**1.** $z = 8$      **2.** $m = -10$      **3.** $y = 10$      **4.** $y = 16$      **5.** $z = 2$      **6.** $x = -20$

**7.** m = -8    **8.** k = 4    **9.** x = -9    **10.** z = 8    **11.** z = 4    **12.** x = -10

**13.** k = 11    **14.** k = 11    **15.** y = 18    **16.** y = -5    **17.** x = -10    **18.** z = 16

**19.** z = -6    **20.** m = 1    **21.** m = 19    **22.** m = 6    **23.** y = 5    **24.** z = -5

**25.** k = 16    **26.** k = 3    **27.** k = 13    **28.** x = 19    **29.** m = -6    **30.** k = 14

**31.** k = -3    **32.** x = 6    **33.** m = -1    **34.** k = 10    **35.** k = -1    **36.** k = -8

**37.** x = 17    **38.** m = 7    **39.** k = 5    **40.** y = -1    **41.** x = -10    **42.** z = -20

**43.** m = 12    **44.** y = 10    **45.** y = -4    **46.** m = 17    **47.** k = 17    **48.** k = -6

**49.** m = -6    **50.** k = 14    **51.** m = 4    **52.** k = -9    **53.** x = 252    **54.** m = 14

**55.** k = 17    **56.** x = 11

**Page 52:   Evaluating Equations**

**1.** 30    **2.** 70    **3.** 15    **4.** 36    **5.** 15    **6.** 10    **7.** 112    **8.** 27

**Page 53:   Evaluating Equations**

**1.** 37    **2.** 82    **3.** -54    **4.** 100    **5.** -16    **6.** 27    **7.** 76    **8.** 77

**Page 54:   Evaluating Equations**

**1.** 27    **2.** -6    **3.** 20    **4.** 14    **5.** 9    **6.** 27    **7.** 29    **8.** 4

**Page 55:   Evaluating Equations**

**1.** 102    **2.** 63    **3.** 7.5    **4.** 74    **5.** 6    **6.** 63    **7.** 33    **8.** 12

**Page 56:   Evaluating Equations**

**1.** 0.7    **2.** 19    **3.** 45    **4.** 35    **5.** 50    **6.** 40    **7.** 44    **8.** 10

**Page 57:   Evaluating Equations**

**1.** 27    **2.** 84    **3.** 16    **4.** 34    **5.** 45    **6.** 6.5    **7.** 34    **8.** 7

**Page 58:   Evaluating Equations**

**1.** 24    **2.** 6.7    **3.** 53    **4.** 52    **5.** 51    **6.** -12    **7.** 51    **8.** -21